A BULB
FOR ALL
SEASONS

How To Grow

A Bulb-a-Month

Indoors

For A Year Of

Flowering

Houseplants

QUIN ELLIS

Illustrations by
BUD PEEN

Hearst Books
New York

PRODUCTIONS

To Herbert Mitgang, master of the bulb, and an inspiration to us all.

Library of Congress Cataloging-in-Publication Data
Ellis, Quin.
A bulb for all seasons: how to grow a bulb-a-month indoors for
a year of flowering houseplants/ by Quin Ellis:
illustrations by Bud Peen — 1st ed.
p. cm
ISBN: 0-688-12412-7
1. Bulbs. 2. Indoor gardening. I. Title.
SB424. E44 1994
635.9'44 — dc20   93-12437
CIP

Printed in Singapore

First Edition

1   3   5   7   9   10   8   6   4   2

Contents

I N T R O D U C T I O N
Parlor Gardening Plain and Simple ❧ *4*

AUTUMN

S E P T E M B E R
Autumn Daffodil ❧ *9*

O C T O B E R
Paper White Narcissus ❧ *13*

N O V E M B E R
Autumn Crocus ❧ *17*

WINTER

D E C E M B E R
Freesia ❧ *23*

J A N U A R Y
Amaryllis ❧ *27*

F E B R U A R Y
Soleil d'Or Narcissus ❧ *31*

SPRING

M A R C H
Hyacinth ❧ *37*

A P R I L
Fools Rose ❧ *41*

M A Y
Lily Of The Valley ❧ *45*

SUMMER

J U N E
Fairy Bells ❧ *51*

J U L Y
Wood Sorrel ❧ *55*

A U G U S T
Meadow Saffron ❧ *59*

B U L B S - B Y - M A I L
Shopping Guide ❧ *62*

Introduction

Welcome to a year-long, indoor flower garden. *A Bulb For All Seasons* is a twelve-month schedule to forcing a bulb a month for beautiful blooming plants in every room of your home throughout the year. Just follow the step-by-step recipes to planting and caring for each bulb, and before the year is half over, you'll be a parlor gardener extraordinaire. Everything you need to know is included: when to order, when to plant, when to water, when to feed, and when to allow your bulb to hibernate for a flowering reincarnation later on.

The blooming calendar is carefully organized so that you're planting your bulbs as soon as you receive them from the nursery or greenhouse listed in the Shopping Guide at the back of the book. Fools Rose, Hyacinth, and Autumn Crocus are stored for several weeks before planting to maintain the blooming bulb-a-month schedule. Most bulbs are available to order in the autumn and in the spring. They are potted as soon as they arrive. If you prefer to shop at a local garden center, be sure to specify pre-chilled or specially prepared bulbs for indoor forcing.

I've suggested some imaginative ways to plant and display each bulb: a basket garden for your Autumn Crocus, a double-decker planting for your Freesias, a horticultural trick to inspire your *Soleil d'Or* to sprout extra stems, a Fools Rose planted in a geode. If you're a traditionalist, however, and don't believe in gilding the lily, you can plant your bulb in the classic clay pot or planter with wonderful results.

Just remember some simple indoor gardening rules: Every container needs drainage; strong, direct sun fades the bulb's colorful flowers; a drop in temperature below fifty degrees slows your bulb's growing cycle; and most important of all, never overwater your bulb. When water drains out the bottom of the container, it's had enough. Here's a good way to ensure you don't kill your flowers with kindness. If your plant is potted in a cachepot without a drainage hole, water it and then lift the pot to feel its weight. The newly watered container is quite heavy. After a day or two, lift it again and feel the difference as the roots drink the moisture. When the container lifts easily it's time to give your plant another drink.

Now go ahead and enjoy your self-contained little miracle. All it needs is tender loving care and the bulb will do the rest. Happy planting to you.

AUTUMN

S E P T E M B E R

Autumn Daffodil

O C T O B E R

Paper White Narcissus

N O V E M B E R

Autumn Crocus

Autumn Daffodil

STERNBERGIA LUTEA

Plant in Mid-August to Bloom in Mid-September

As summer wanes and spring's "true" daffodils are months away, enjoy the sunny brightness of this charming plant. Each Autumn Daffodil grows five perky yellow flowers on stems six to eight inches high. Plant at least ten bulbs in a rectangular cachepot and your reward will be a flowering carpet of up to fifty golden blossoms! With the right care, your Autumn Daffodils will sparkle with blooms for two weeks.

Autumn Daffodil

The Bulb

A member of the Amaryllis family, the Autumn Daffodil measures
an inch and one-half in diameter. Order ten *Sternbergia* bulbs
in July for mid-August planting.

The Autumn Daffodil Container

A near-square or rectangular ceramic cachepot, seven inches long
with a four- to five-inch depth, for a showy carpet planting.

Planting Autumn Daffodils

Rich potting soil mixed three parts earth to one part sharp sand
for quick drainage. If your cachepot lacks drainage, place a
one-inch layer of pebbles in the bottom to prevent the roots
from rotting. Fill halfway to the top with soil. Place two rows
of five bulbs about an inch apart. Cover with soil to fill the
cachepot. To start, give your Autumn Daffodils a generous
cup of water to saturate the new soil without overdoing it.

Light

Start your Autumn Daffodils in a dark location to allow the roots to
develop. After seven days, move your plant to a permanent home
where it can catch bright, direct sun shining in a southern or western
window. Rotate once a day to prevent the stems
from bending toward the light.

Autumn Daffodil

Temperature

Autumn Daffodils thrive in the warmest room in your house.
A temperature of seventy degrees will keep
the flowers feisty.

Water And Food

Your Autumn Daffodils like evenly moist soil, but not wet.
Water every five to six days. A drink of quarter-strength
liquid plant food once, midway through
the growing cycle, makes generous flowers.

After The Bloom Is Over

The Autumn Daffodil's spiky green foliage is attractive
enough to display after the flowers are gone. When the
leaves die back, remove them, and allow the soil to dry out.
Let the bulbs sleep in darkness for at least two months and
new sprouts will appear. Return your cachepot to a warm,
sunny place, resume watering, and your plant will bloom
again. The Autumn Daffodil successfully repeats the
hibernation/reincarnation cycle to give you
years of lovely flowers.

Paper White Narcissus

N A R C I S S U S   T A Z E T T A

Plant in Early September to Bloom in Mid-October

Fragrant and fruitful, it's no
surprise Paper Whites are a parlor gardener's best friend.
Force three bulbs simply on a bed of smooth pebbles
with a few inches of fresh water to kiss their
squat bottoms. Your Paper Whites' slender stalks
rise elegantly out of abundant foliage to reach a
height of about eighteen inches. The stems support
small bouquets of star-shaped flowers,
scenting your home for two weeks with
their distinctive perfume.

13

Paper White Narcissus

The Bulb

A member of the Amaryllis family, the Paper White measures an inch and one-half in diameter. Order three Narcissus bulbs in August for a triumphant house planting in early September.

The Paper White Container

Virtually any shape, size, and kind of glass or ceramic container keeps your Paper Whites in good humor. The only requirement is a depth of at least two inches with enough surface area to place the bulbs close to each other, but not touching.

Planting Paper Whites

Place two inches of polished medium-size stones in the bottom of your container. Large glass marbles are a fun alternative. Sit the bulbs on top of the stones, about one-half inch apart. Press them down gently to snuggle securely in place. Add enough cool, fresh water to cover the stones and just touch the base of the bulbs.

Light

Start the bulbs off slowly in a dark spot for two to three weeks until you see a well-developed root system and the leaves reach a height of three inches. Then move your Paper Whites to their permanent home in a room with a southern exposure to relish bright, but indirect, light.

Paper White Narcissus

Temperature

An average room temperature varying between sixty and seventy
degrees is ideal for happy Paper Whites.

Water And Food

Maintain a water level that covers the stones to just touch the base
of the bulbs. Paper Whites become spongy and malfunction if
allowed to sit in deep water. Locked inside this bulb is a perfect
botanical clock that time-releases
all the nutrients it needs to perform beautifully.
Feeding is not necessary.

After The Bloom Is Over

Bulbs grown in water don't bloom again indoors for you. The
good news is, Paper Whites flower anew if you replant them
outdoors. After the blossoms fade, lift the bulbs from their water
bed, green leaves and all, to replant in the ground for fresh foliage
in the spring and flowers a year later.

Autumn Crocus

C R O C U S   S P E C I O S U S

Plant in Early October to Bloom in Mid-November

An English trug basket
packed to bursting with Autumn Crocus is
the delight of indoor gardeners in every clime.
Each pert purple cuplet tops a six-inch stem and
presents you with blooms for two jubilant weeks.
The shiny foliage waits patiently for the
flowering cycle to finish before
it makes a genial appearance, extending the
display life of your portable
cottage garden.

Autumn Crocus

The Bulb

A member of the Iris family, the Autumn Crocus measures one inch in diameter. Order twelve to sixteen corms in July for delivery in August or September. Since the seasonal schedule calls for an early October planting, store the corms in a paper bag in a cool, dry place until it's time to let them grow.

The Autumn Crocus Container

The trug, a shallow wood-slatted basket with a high arching handle, is a terrific way to grow a chummy flower bed of Autumn Crocus. Select one about twelve inches long with a four-inch depth.

Planting Autumn Crocus

Rich potting soil mixed three parts earth to one part sharp sand for quick drainage. To prevent soil from falling through the trug's open weave, but without inhibiting drainage, line the bottom and sides of the basket with a double layer of cheesecloth. Fill the basket halfway to the top with soil. Place two rows of corms down the center, lengthwise, with two inches between the rows. Avoid planting directly under the basket handle. Cozy the corms right next to each other. Cover with a generous inch of soil. Complete your blooming basket with curly strands of Spanish moss tucked around the edges to conceal any exposed cheesecloth.

Water well to soak through.

Autumn Crocus

Light

Bright and indirect. Situate your Autumn Crocus in a room with a southern exposure where strong, but indirect, light keeps the purple flowers at maximum vibrancy.

Temperature

Like its friend the Autumn Daffodil, the Autumn Crocus flourishes in the warmest room in your house. A room temperature of seventy degrees stimulates hearty blossoms.

Water And Food

Your Autumn Crocus prefers evenly moist soil. Water every five to six days. A light feeding of quarter-strength liquid plant food once, midway through the growing cycle, is appreciated.

After The Bloom Is Over

Autumn Crocus hangs-dry beautifully. Snip the stems of the fully opened flowers, gather them in bunches, tie together, and suspend the bouquets upside down in a warm, dry place. The plants' grasslike leaves live on for several weeks after you harvest the flowers. When the leaves complete their pretty display, dig out the hard-working corms and check their condition. If they're still plump and hard, plant them outdoors for others to enjoy next year; if soft and shriveled, sorrowfully discard them.

WINTER

BLOOMS

DECEMBER

Freesia

JANUARY

Amaryllis

FEBRUARY

Soleil d'Or Narcissus

Freesia

FREESIA X HYBRIDA

Plant in Mid-October to Bloom in Mid-December

Deck the halls with
a magnificent double-decker planting of
sweetly scented Freesia. *Winter Gold,* one of
the yellow varieties, is especially fragrant. Each corm
grows a lithe stem as tall as two feet that
gracefully arcs under the weight of eight
buttercup bugles. Enjoy the floral aria as each
flower bud waits its turn in line before bursting
into bloom. A bas-relief terra-cotta planter
is the classic stage for a three-week run
of flowering Freesia.

Freesia

The Bulb

A member of the Iris family, the *Winter Gold* measures an inch and one-half in diameter. Order a dozen corms, specially prepared for forcing indoors, in early September for a mid-October planting.

The Freesia Container

A rectangular terra-cotta planter, eight inches long with a five- to six-inch depth, easily accommodates your double-decker layer of corms.

Planting Freesia

Rich potting soil mixed three parts earth to one part sharp sand for quick drainage. To prevent soil from falling through, but without inhibiting drainage, place a few pebbles or a piece of broken pottery over the hole in the bottom of the container. Fill nearly half the container with soil. Place a zigzag row of six corms one-half inch apart. Cover with two inches of soil. Place the second tier of six corms to zigzag in the opposite direction. Cover with a generous inch of soil. Water well to soak through. While you wait for the reluctant Freesias to bloom, give your plant a seasonal touch: Decorate the naked soil with a handful of cranberries and some well-placed kumquats.

Freesia

Light

Start your Freesia in a cold, dark place. After seven days, leaves begin to sprout and it's time to move your plant to a permanent home where it can catch bright, direct light shining in a southern or western window. Should any of the delicate stems topple, gently support them on slender stakes.

Temperature

Freesia is particularly finicky. Before first sprouts appear, it favors a chilly temperature varying between fifty and sixty degrees. Thereafter, to grow buoyant, heavily scented blooms, it prefers the contrast of a seventy degree daytime temperature with a nighttime temperature drop of ten to fifteen degrees.

Water And Food

Keep Freesia evenly moist, but not wet. Water it every five to six days. Three weeks after the leaves appear, your Freesia welcomes a light feeding of quarter-strength liquid plant food.

After The Bloom Is Over

When the flowers fade and the leaves yellow, dig out the corms for inspection. The ones that are firm and/or producing cormlets you can replant outside to flower again in the spring.

Amaryllis

HIPPEASTRUM

Plant in Early December to Bloom in Mid-January

The wonderful Amaryllis
bursts forth with immense, trumpet-shaped
blooms to herald the start of a new year.
Place the velvety *Red Lion* in a sunny
spot and watch it sprout two strong
stems up to two feet high with four plump
buds perched atop each. Plant your Amaryllis
in a colorful cachepot to display a
month of eye-popping flowers.

Amaryllis

The Bulb

A member of the Amaryllis family, the *Red Lion* measures three inches in diameter. Order one bulb in November to plant with fanfare in early December.

The Amaryllis Container

The bolder the better is first choice for a ceramic cachepot to grow your striking Amaryllis. A perfect fit is six inches in diameter and five inches deep.

Planting Amaryllis

Rich potting soil mixed three parts earth to one part sharp sand for quick drainage. If your elegant cachepot lacks drainage, place a one-inch layer of pebbles in the bottom to prevent the roots from rotting. Fill halfway to the top with soil. Position the bulb in the center. Pack soil around the bulb to hold it snugly in place, but don't cover it. Leave the top third exposed to air and light. To start, give your Amaryllis a cup of water to saturate the new soil without overwatering. It's not unusual for a contented Amaryllis to produce a second, and sometimes a third, stem of blooms. Cut the stems back as the flowers fade, and continue care.

Light

Bright and direct. Situate your Amaryllis to catch the sun shining

Amaryllis

through a southern or western window. Rotate your plant to prevent the stems from bending toward the light. The flowers last longer if you pinch out the anthers of the newly opened blossoms.

Temperature

Amaryllis appreciates an average room temperature varying between sixty and seventy degrees.

Water And Food

Your Amaryllis lives in evenly moist soil. Water it every five to six days. A light feeding of quarter-strength liquid plant food, once midway through the growing cycle, will make this *Red Lion* roar!

After The Bloom Is Over

For months, after the last stem blooms, the foliage is green and growing. Continue care with additional feedings of quarter-strength liquid plant food every other time you water to pack the bulb with nutrients for its hibernation. When the foliage yellows, stop watering and store the cachepot in a cool, dark place for six to eight weeks. New sprouts will show themselves. Scrape away the top inch of soil and replace with a fresh layer. Return to a sunny spot, resume watering, and your Amaryllis will flower again. The Amaryllis successfully repeats the hibernation/reincarnation cycle and gladly blooms for years.

Soleil d'Or Narcissus

NARCISSUS TAZETTA

Plant in Late December to Bloom in Mid-February

Pander to the vanity of this jaunty flower. Plant a single *Soleil d'Or* in a Grecian urn to honor its mythological roots. With a trick of parlor-gardening magic, your Narcissus gives you a bonus of three to six extra blossoming stems. Each graceful, foot-tall stem is crowned with a coronet of burnished gold and sun-yellow chalice-shaped flora. *Soleil d'Or* blooms for two glorious weeks, scenting your home with its dreamy fragrance.

$S\,o\,l\,e\,i\,l\ \ d\,'O\,r$ Narcissus

The Bulb

A member of the Amaryllis family, the *Soleil d'Or* measures three inches in diameter, twice the size of its little sister, the Paper White. Order one bulb in November for planting after Christmas.

The *Soleil d'Or* Container

Feel free to be adventurous in your choice of cachepot for the freewheeling *Soleil d'Or*. A container five inches in diameter with a five-inch depth is all you need, the bulb does the rest!

Planting *Soleil d'Or*

Rich potting soil is perfect, no need to add sand to force a very willing *Soleil d'Or*. Of course, good drainage is a standard requirement. If your cachepot is lacking, place a one-inch layer of pebbles at the bottom of the cachepot. Fill with two inches of soil. Before you plant your bulb, try this horticultural trick to force three to six extra stems in addition to the bulb's already bountiful bouquet. Using a sharp knife, make two inch-long horizontal incisions, opposite each other, curving around the belly of the bulb. Imagine you are cutting into the skin of an onion. Place the bulb in the center of the container. Fill in snugly with soil all around. Cover the tip with a shy inch. For its first drink, give your *Soleil d'Or* a cup of water to saturate the new soil without overdoing it.

Soleil d'Or Narcissus

Light

Start your plant off slowly in a dark place to promote strong
roots and sturdy stems. After three weeks, move your
Soleil d'Or to its permanent home in a room with a southern
exposure to luxuriate in bright, but indirect, light. Rotate your
plant to prevent the stems from bending toward the light. You
may need to use thin stakes for support.

Temperature

Your *Soleil d'Or* will reach its potential in an average room
temperature varying between sixty and seventy degrees.

Water And Food

Keep your plant evenly moist, but not wet. Water every five
to six days. After the leaves sprout, feed it with
quarter-strength liquid plant food twice during the five
weeks it grows to bloom.

After The Bloom Is Over

After the flowers fade, dig the bulb out of the soil. Check its
condition. If hearty and hard, plant it outdoors to grow
leaves next spring and to grow flowers the following
year and for years to come.

SPRING

BLOOMS

MARCH

Hyacinth

APRIL

Fools Rose

MAY

Lily Of The Valley

Hyacinth

HYACINTHUS ORIENTALIS

Plant in Mid-January to Bloom in Mid-March

Victorian parlor gardeners
so admired the fresh fragrance of Hyacinth,
they invented a special hourglass-shaped
container in its honor. The Hyacinth Glass is
still the premier showcase for this miracle of
growth. The dainty *Anne Marie* may try your
patience, but when her praying hands
of thick foliage open to a cone-shaped colony
of bright florets, stretching silvery pink
toward the sun, your reward is
two weeks of stately bloom.

Hyacinth

The Bulb

A member of the Lily family, the *Anne Marie* measures an inch and
one-half in diameter. Order one bulb, or more if you like, specially
pre-chilled for forcing indoors, in late November for delivery in late
December. Since the seasonal schedule calls for a mid-January
planting, store the bulb in a paper bag in your refrigerator
until it's time to let it grow.

The Hyacinth Container

A Hyacinth Glass is *comme il faut.* This classic container is found at
your local nursery or by mail from a catalog, or you may spot a
vintage one in an antiques shop or at a flea market.
They're highly collectible.

Planting Hyacinth

Fill the Hyacinth Glass to its "waist" with water. Place your bulb to
sit perfectly in the cup made especially for it, the water
just caressing the bulb's base.

Light

Start your Hyacinth in a dark corner to grow strong roots three
inches long. After three weeks, move your plant to its permanent
home in a room with southern or western exposure to catch bright,
direct sunshine. Rotate your plant for uniform flower development.

Hyacinth

Temperature

Hyacinth feels right at home in an average room temperature varying between sixty and seventy degrees.

Water And Food

Maintain a water level to cover and nourish the roots, but just to touch the base of the bulb. As your Hyacinth grows, a lively ecosystem develops in the glass. The roots look velvety and soft, the water cloudy. Don't be alarmed; it's a natural part of the growing process. Your plant looks forward to a pick-me-up of quarter-strength liquid plant food midway through the growing cycle.

After The Bloom Is Over

A dutiful Hyacinth, water-forced indoors, can *sometimes* be replanted outside with good results. Check the condition of the bulb. If it's hale and hearty, not shriveled and spent, plant it in the ground to flower again next spring.

Fools Rose

R H O D O H Y P O X I S   B A U R

Plant in Late February to Bloom in Early April

It's hard to sit by and
allow this spirited, parlor-friendly plant to be called
Rhodohypoxis. The "rose" red flower is so genial and
energetic that a reward was in order. We christened it
Fools Rose after the Greek name Rhodon, meaning "rose."
Let's hope the name catches on.
In the meantime, use its official nomenclature,
Rhodohypoxis, when you order it. Mass plant a crowd of
fifteen Fools Rose to reap cute bunches of
magenta flowers, standing on tiptoe
over small beds of fuzzy foliage
for two whole months of baby blooms.

Fools Rose

The Bulb

The only member of the *Rhodohypoxis* family, the Fools Rose
measures one-quarter to one-half inch in diameter. Order
fifteen red *Rhodohypoxis* rhizomes in early December for
delivery after Christmas week. Since the seasonal schedule
calls for a late February planting, store the rhizomes in a
paper bag in a cool, dark place until it's time to let them grow.

The Fools Rose Container

A squat, ceramic planter, five inches in diameter with a four-
inch depth, is ideal for a chockablock planting.

Planting Fools Rose

Rich potting soil mixed three parts earth to one part sharp
sand for quick drainage. To prevent soil from falling through,
but without inhibiting drainage, place a few pebbles or a piece
of broken pottery over the hole in the bottom of the planter.
Fill nearly three-quarters of the planter with soil. Place the
rhizomes close, but not touching. Start in the center and work
your way out, in concentric circles, to plant one inch from the
rim all around. Cover with a shy inch of soil. Water
well to soak through. Finish with a thin layer of white
sand to cover and decorate.

Fools Rose

Light

Bright and indirect. Situate your Fools Rose in a room with a southern exposure where it grows in strong, but indirect, light. Rotate the plant for uniform flower development.

Temperature

Fools Rose favors an average room temperature varying between sixty and seventy degrees.

Water And Food

Your Fools Rose likes moist soil. A drink of water every four days keeps the roots nourished, but not soggy. A light feeding of quarter-strength liquid plant food, every other time you water, replenishes your hard-working plant during the two months it diligently produces flowers for you.

After The Bloom Is Over

When the flowers fade and the leaves yellow, allow the soil to dry out. Store the planter of sleeping rhizomes in a cool, sunless spot for three months, then return your Fools Rose to a light-filled place, resume watering, and your little plant will greet the world with new resolve. Fools Rose repeats the hibernation/reincarnation cycle for years of rosy blooms.

Lily Of The Valley

CONVALLARIA MAJALIS

Plant in Mid-April to Bloom in Mid-May

In the language of flowers,
Lily Of The Valley says happiness. Coy blossoms,
lots of foliage, lovely Lily trembles with romance.
Plant an angelic cascade of ladies-in-
waiting to hang on your wall in a ceramic sconce.
Each pip will grow a single stem six inches tall,
wearing a tassel of tiny white wedding bells.
For three weeks your Lily Of The Valley
corsage is in bloom, faithfully
emitting its sweet scent.

Lily Of The Valley

The Bulb

A member of the Lily family, the Lily Of The Valley measures one-quarter to one-half inch in length. Order a dozen pre-chilled rhizomes, known as pips, in March for planting a merry nosegay in mid-April.

The Lily Of The Valley Container

A terra-cotta wall sconce and a fragrant bouquet of Lily Of The Valley is a marriage made in heaven. Select one about eight inches long by five inches wide and deep. To protect your wall, choose a sconce without drainage.

Planting Lily Of The Valley

Rich potting soil is ideal, no need to add sand into the growing mix for these willing lovelies. Place a one-inch layer of tiny pebbles in the bottom of the sconce. Fill with three inches of soil. Place the twelve pips, one inch apart, in three rows thus: back row, five pips; middle row, four pips; front row, three pips. Cover all with a generous inch of soil. To start, give your Lily Of The Valley a generous cup of water to saturate the soil.

Light

Bright. Situate your Lily Of The Valley in a room with an eastern exposure to catch morning brightness, but indirect light for most of the day. Don't let its innocent appearance fool you. Lily Of The Valley is poisonous, so keep children and pets out of harm's way.

Temperature

An average room temperature varying between sixty and seventy degrees is agreeable.

Water And Food

Lily Of The Valley likes moist soil. Water every four days. Touch the terra-cotta sconce to test for dryness. If it feels damp and cool, it's still nicely moist; if dry and room temperature, it's time to water. Feed with quarter-strength liquid plant food, midway through the growing cycle.

After The Bloom Is Over

Lily Of The Valley makes a wonderful keepsake. Harvest sprigs of flowers to press for personalizing stationery or decorating seasonal gifts. After the blossoms are gone, the leaves continue to give pleasure for another six weeks and may present you with a blessing of red berries. The pips can be replanted outdoors, in cold winter climates, to flower next spring.

SUMMER

J U N E

Fairy Bells

J U L Y

Wood Sorrel

A U G U S T

Meadow Saffron

Fairy Bells

MELASPHAERULA RAMOSA (GRAMINEA)

Plant in Early May to Bloom in Mid-June

The crazy-quilt tangle
of tiny white and purple sprites,
dancing willy-nilly on wily
eighteen-inch stems, is a spring fever dream.
Mass plant a woodland carpet of
Fairy Bells to stand tall in an
umbrella holder, mocking last month's
showers with this month's flowers.

Fairy Bells

The Bulb

A member of the Iris family, Fairy Bells measures one-half inch in diameter. Order fifteen black *Melasphaerula* corms at the end of March for an early May planting.

The Fairy Bells Container

Show off your willowy grove of Fairy Bells by inserting a ceramic planter inside an umbrella stand pedestal. Extra height is counterpoint to the whimsy of twining flowers and curling foliage. A squat ceramic planter, seven inches in diameter with a five-inch depth, sitting in a nine-inch saucer, is perfect for this vertical meadowland planting. Choose an umbrella stand two feet tall with an inside diameter of ten inches to house your planter and saucer.

Planting Fairy Bells

Rich potting soil mixed three parts earth to one part sharp sand for quick drainage. To prevent soil from falling through, but without inhibiting drainage, place a few pebbles or a piece of broken pottery over the hole in the bottom of the planter. Fill nearly two-thirds with soil. Place the corms close, but not touching. Start in the center and work your way out, in concentric circles, to plant one inch from the rim all around. Cover with a shy inch of soil. Water well to soak through. Fill

Fairy Bells

the umbrella stand with fourteen inches of popped popcorn, tightly packed. Two thirty-two ounce packages of unpopped corn should yield enough. Place the planter and saucer in the umbrella stand to sit securely atop the ledge of popcorn.

Light

Bright and direct. Situate your Fairy Bells to catch the sun shining through a southern or western window. Rotate your plant to prevent it from bending toward the light.

Temperature

An average room temperature varying between sixty and seventy degrees will keep your Fairy Bells ringing.

Water And Food

Fairy Bells prefers its soil on the dry side. Water every six to seven days. Lightly feed with quarter-strength liquid plant food every two weeks.

After The Bloom Is Over

When the flowers fade and the leaves yellow, allow the soil to dry out. Store your planter in cool darkness for three months, then return it to a sunny place, resume watering, and it will bloom anew. Fairy Bells repeats the hibernation/reincarnation cycle to flower season after season.

Wood Sorrel

O X A L I S   D E P P E I

Plant in Late May to Bloom in Mid-July

Wood Sorrel is your
devoted companion when other indoor-friendly
bulbs are out of town. Choose wonderful
Iron Cross for puckered clusters of
floral pink kisses all summer long. Plant a lush
forest lawn of a dozen pea-size bulbs inside
the hollow of a crosscut geode.
The natural mineral environment inspires
each tiny bulb to sprout four rich green clover
leaves growing in the shade of a hot pink
six-sided parasol of flowers.

W o o d S o r r e l

The Bulb

A member of the Oxalis family, Wood Sorrel measures one-quarter to one-half inch in diameter. Order a dozen pea-size *Oxalis deppei* bulbs in April for a late May planting. Specify the *Iron Cross* variety, bursting with bright pink blossoms and a bevy of lucky clover leaves.

The Wood Sorrel Container

A petite bulb, Wood Sorrel is naturally cozy growing inside the hollow of a crosscut semiprecious mineral rock. Choose a geode with a large cavelike opening, five inches in diameter with a four-inch depth.

Planting Wood Sorrel

Rich potting soil mixed three parts earth to one part sharp sand for quick drainage is home sweet home. Fill three-quarters of the geode with soil. Place the bulbs about one inch apart. Start in the center and work your way out, in concentric circles, to plant one inch from the rim all around. Cover with a shy inch of soil. For its first drink, give your Wood Sorrel one-quarter cup of water to saturate the soil without overwatering.

Light

Start your Wood Sorrel off slowly in a dark place. After a few

W o o d S o r r e l

days, leaf tips appear and it's time to move your plant to a
permanent home in a room with southern exposure where it
thrives in bright, but indirect, light. At night, the light-sensitive
flowers twirl to close like a parasol. As the sun rises, watch the
blossoms unfurl to greet a new day.

Temperature

An average room temperature varying between sixty
and seventy degrees is correct.

Water And Food

Wood Sorrel likes its soil on the dry side. Water every six to
seven days. After the foliage appears, supplement with a light
feeding of quarter-strength liquid plant food every two weeks.

After The Bloom Is Over

Enjoy your Wood Sorrel's clover and honey-spot leaves after the
flowers fade. When they too are gone, store your geode out of
light to rest the bulbs. After three months, return the geode to a
light-filled place and resume watering. Wood Sorrel graciously
repeats the hibernation/reincarnation cycle for years
of floral laureates.

Meadow Saffron

COLCHICUM AUTUMNALE

Plant in Mid-August to Bloom in Late August

Here's one for the books.
The amazing Meadow Saffron flowers like topsy
without soil or water! Give this air plant
some bright light and it blossoms in just a
few days. You can count on the gay *Water Lily*
for six or more short-stemmed lavender-and-white
blooms that fan like the plumage on a tiny tropical bird.
Perch a flock of Meadow Saffron on the ledges of an
antique birdcage and watch it preen its
feathery petals for the two weeks
it's in full bloom.

Meadow Saffron

The Bulb

A member of the Lily family, Meadow Saffron measures
three inches in length. Order three or more
jumbo *Colchicum autumnale* corms in July
for a mid-August planting. Specify the
Water Lily variety for cocky lavender-and-white tail feathers.

The Meadow Saffron Container

A wood or wicker birdcage becomes a Meadow Saffron
aviary. Choose one with three stable ledges or
platforms to perch a bulb on each.
If you are birdless, and desire to remain so,
your Meadow Saffron grows on a bookshelf,
in a seashell or brandy snifter, or cradled in a basket.
Use your imagination.

Planting Meadow Saffron

Place your Meadow Saffron in a congenial environment and the
unconventional bulb grows without being "planted."

Light

Bright and indirect. Situate your Meadow Saffron
in a room with southern exposure, where it grows in spite
of you, in bright, but indirect, light.

Meadow Saffron

Rotate to prevent the feathery flowers from leaning
toward the light. A word of caution:
Meadow Saffron is poisonous, so keep away
from tiny hands and paws.

Water And Food

Fresh air is the only nutrient your Meadow Saffron needs to
perform to perfection.

After The Bloom Is Over

When the flowers wither, replant your Meadow Saffron
outdoors for new foliage in the spring and
flowers again in the summer.

Shopping Guide

B u l b s - b y - M a i l

*A mail-order source guide to specially prepared or
pre-chilled bulbs, corms, and rhizomes from the best
nurseries, greenhouses, and indoor-garden catalogs*

Carman's Garden
16201 East Mozart Avenue
Los Gatos, CA 95032
(408) 356-0119
✤ Fools Rose
(Rhodohypoxis baurii)

The Daffodil Mart
Route 3, Box 794
Gloucester, VA 23061
(804) 693-3966
✤ Fairy Bells; Hyacinth;
Meadow Saffron *(Colchicum
autumnale)*; Paper White
Narcissus; Wood Sorrel
(Oxalis deppei)

David Kay Catalog
One Jenni Lane
Peoria, IL 61614
(800) 535-9917
✤ Indoor-garden supplies

Gardeners Eden Catalog
P.O. Box 7307
San Francisco, CA 94120
(800) 822-9600
✤ Indoor-garden supplies

Shopping Guide

Gardenimport Inc.
P.O. Box 760
Thornhill, Ontario L3T 4A5
Canada
(416) 731-1950
↬ Autumn Crocus; Freesia;
Meadow Saffron *(Colchicum autumnale)*

Green Lady Gardens
1415 Eucalyptus Drive
San Francisco, CA 94132
(415) 753-3332
↬ Autumn Daffodil; Fairy
Bells; Fools Rose
(Rhodohypoxis baurii);
Meadow Saffron *(Colchicum autumnale)*; Wood Sorrel
(Oxalis deppei)

Greer Gardens
1280 Goodpasture Island Road
Eugene, OR 97401
(503) 686-8266
↬ Fools Rose
(Rhodohypoxis baurii)

McClure and Zimmerman
P.O. Box 368
Friesland, WI 53935
(414) 326-4220
↬ Amaryllis; Autumn Crocus;
Autumn Daffodil; Meadow
Saffron *(Colchicum autumnale)*

Roberta Fortune's Catalog
150 Chestnut Street
San Francisco, CA 94111
(800) 331-2300
↬ Indoor-garden supplies

Smith and Hawken Catalog
25 Corte Madera
Mill Valley, CA 94941
(415) 383-2000
✣ Amaryllis; Freesia; Paper White and *Soleil d'Or* Narcissus; indoor-garden supplies

Solutions Catalog
P.O. Box 6878
Portland, OR 97228
(800) 342-9988
✣ Indoor-garden supplies

Van Bourgondien
245 Farmingdale Road
P.O. Box A
Babylon, NY 11702
(516) 669-3500
✣ Freesia; Hyacinth; Lily Of The Valley

Wayside Gardens
1 Garden Lane
Hodges, SC 29695
(800) 845-1124
✣ Amaryllis; Autumn Crocus; Freesia; Hyacinth; Meadow Saffron *(Colchicum autumnale)*

White Flower Farm
30 Irene Street
Torrington, CT 06790
(800) 944-9624
✣ Fools Rose *(Rhodohypoxis baurii)*; Lily Of The Valley; *Soleil d'Or* Narcissus; Wood Sorrel *(Oxalis deppei)*